© Copyright 2020 by **Riddleland** - All rights reserved.

The content contained within this book may not be reproduced, duplicated or transmitted without direct written permission from the author or the publisher.

Under no circumstances will any blame or legal responsibility be held against the publisher, or author, for any damages, reparation, or monetary loss due to the information contained within this book, either directly or indirectly.

Legal Notice:

This book is copyright protected. It is only for personal use. You cannot amend, distribute, sell, use, quote or paraphrase any part, or the content within this book, without the consent of the author or publisher.

Disclaimer Notice:

Please note the information contained within this document is for educational and entertainment purposes only. All effort has been executed to present accurate, up to date, reliable, complete information. No warranties of any kind are declared or implied. Readers acknowledge that the author is not engaged in the rendering of legal, financial, medical or professional advice. The content within this book has been derived from various sources.

Design by freepik.com

Table of Contents

In a world in which three-leaf clovers are the norm, finding a four-leaf clover means that one is extremely lucky. Each leaf of the four-leaf clover is distinct, and yet all are part of the clover and without it the clover would be incomplete.

This book is not your normal joke book. Like the clover, it is broken into four sections, called leaves; each leaf contributes to make the resulting unit a whole. The leaves are question-and-answer jokes, puns, silly situations, and knock-knock jokes.

Leaf One: Question and Answer Jokes   pg 8

Leaf Two: Puns   pg 48

Leaf Three: Silly Scenarios and Words of Wisdom   pg 75

Leaf Four: Knock-Knock Jokes   pg 84

Did you enjoy the book?   pg 98

Bonus   pg 99

Contest   pg 100

Other books by Riddleland   pg 101

About Riddleland   pg 105

Riddleland Bonus Book

http://pixelfy.me/riddlelandbonus

Thank you for buying this book. We would like to share a special bonus as a token of appreciation. It is a collection of 50 original jokes, riddles, and two super funny stories!

Join our **Facebook Group** at **Riddleland for Kids** to get daily jokes and riddles.

Introduction

May your pockets be heavy and your heart be light, may good luck pursue you each morning and night. ~ **Irish blessing**

Get ready to laugh! **It's Laugh O'Clock Joke Book: Lucky Clover Edition** is different from other joke books. This book is not meant to be read alone - although it can be; instead it is a game to be played with siblings, friends, family or between two people to see who can make the other laugh first. It's time to laugh; it's always laugh o'clock somewhere.

These jokes are written to provide a fun, quality reading experience. Children learn best when they are playing; reading is fun when it is something one wants to read, and most children want to read jokes. Reading jokes will increase vocabulary and comprehension. Jokes also have many other benefits:

- **Bonding** – Sharing this book is an excellent way for parents and children to spend some quality time having fun, sharing laughs, and making memories.

- **Building Confidence** - When parents ask one of the jokes, it creates a safe environment for children to burst out answers even if they are incorrect. This helps children to develop self-confidence and self-expression.

- **Improve Vocabulary** - Jokes are a lot of fun, and that makes reading a lot of fun. Children will need to understand the words if they want to understand the jokes.

- **Enhancing Reading Comprehension** - Many children can read at a young age but may not understand the context of words in the sentences. Jokes, especially puns, can help develop children's interest to comprehend the context.

- **Developing Creativity** - Funny, creative jokes can help children develop their sense of humor while getting their brains working. Many times a word in a joke can be taken two ways, and picturing it both ways leads to creative imagery.

- **Developing Logical Thinking Skills** - Because many jokes have a dual play on words, children must use logic to decide which meaning the speaker intended.

Enjoy the book, and, remember, it's always laugh o'clock somewhere.

FUN FACTS FOR ST PATRICK'S DAY

Where do you think St. Patrick was originally from?

Many people would assume Ireland. But, he was from Britain, and it's not certain if he was born in Wales or Scotland.

Do you know why the lucky three-leafed shamrock is associated with St. Patrick?

It is said that he used the shamrock as a symbol to represent the Holy Trinity when he introduced Christianity to Ireland.

LEAF ONE
Question and Answer Jokes

"I have noticed that timing and luck sometimes line up in such a way that you can catch a break."
~ **Ellie Kemper**

Maybe things didn't happen quite like the joke answer says that they happened, but the issues raised will hopefully make you curious to learn about St. Patrick and about the lore of leprechauns, rainbows, and pots of gold.

St. Patrick was a real person. He was a Christian missionary in Ireland. Because the average person could not read, St. Patrick taught the people about the Trinity by using a three leaf clover; he showed that it had three distinct leaves and yet formed one whole. The lore that surrounds St Patrick is likely built on some factual events. One of his most famous events is driving out the snakes because they were annoying him - even today, if you see a snake in the church sanctuary you aren't likely to be able to focus on worshipping - so the lore of his driving out snakes probably has truth to it as well.

Lucky Clover Edition

Everybody should learn about St. Patrick sometime, so what better way to get introduced to him and to Irish lore – leprechauns, sprites, and pots of gold - than through humor such as this:

How long are the leprechaun's legs?

Just long enough to touch the ground.

How are the jokes in this book like the pot of coins at the end of the rainbow?

Both are pure gold.

How do you encourage a leprechaun who is jogging back to his house?

"Go, gnome."

What do you call facts about leprechauns that are not public knowledge?

Little gnome facts.

What did the shoe making leprechaun say when he realized that the actor's shoe was the wrong size?

"The shoe must go on!"

Looking up at the rainbow, I can see yellow; why isn't there gold in the rainbow?

The gold is all in a pot at the end.

Why did the leprechaun play his fiddle inside the refrigerator?

He wanted to play cool tunes.

Lucky Clover Edition

What does Ireland have more of than any other country in the world?

Irish citizens.

What did the self-centered person say on St. Patrick's Day?

"Who needs luck? I've got charm."

Do you realize most people own as much gold as they do silver?

(They don't have any of either.)

How did the leprechaun break the news to the treasure hunter who came upon him that there wasn't any gold at the end of the rainbow?

"Perhaps there is gold at the end of the rainbow, but this isn't the end – this is the beginning."

Leprechauns are smaller than a pod of peas, but they dress fancy; what kind of suit did the leprechaun get?

A three-peas suit.

Why do leprechauns wear hats instead of scarves?

Scarves are something they just can't wrap their head around.

What is the study of leprechaun society called?

Gnomenclature.

Why did the gold-digging leprechaun want to be left alone?

He was mining his own business.

What do a leprechaun who is building an underground home and a bad author have in common?

Both have lots of holes in their plots.

Lucky Clover Edition

What kind of snake built a home in Ireland before St. Patrick came along?

A boa constructor.

Why did St. Patrick not leave even one female snake behind?

Because that would have been a miss snake (mistake).

Why did the priest leave his shoes out for the leprechaun cobbler?

His shoes needed healing.

Why should you not eat popcorn at the movie theater while watching a horror movie featuring a leprechaun?

The popcorn will leave a film in your mouth.

What happened when a kid named David snuck upon the magic, mischievous trickster leprechaun, captured him under a clothesbasket, and demanded, "I want to be rich"?

The leprechaun changed his name to Rich.

What is the name of the famous Irish skeptic?

O' Really.

How do leprechauns saw down four-leaf clovers?

With four-leaf cleavers.

What does the nasty purple mark one gets when bumping one's self have in common with the leprechaun's tea recipe?

Both are nasty brews.

Who helps the leprechaun construct his underground home?

The hole family.

Lucky Clover Edition

When asked if he liked making his underground home, what did the leprechaun say?

"I dig it."

Why did the sad leprechaun hate being a cobbler?

He found it sole destroying.

What do you call two leprechauns making shoes as a human cobbler would?

Pair of normal activity.

How do you measure a snake?

Use either metric or inches; snakes don't have feet.

What roles did the leprechaun usually play on the baseball team?

He played shortstop and was the pinch runner.

Rudolph is the most famous deer of the Christmas season; which deer will you likely hear mentioned on St. Patrick's Day?

"O' Deer (Oh, dear.)".

Why do people who don't like green still wear it on St. Patrick's Day?

If they don't wear it, they will likely find themselves in a pinch.

What did Dad say when he woke up wearing a goofy leprechaun outfit complete with a green bowler?

"I think I look funny; I think I slept funny."

What did people say when the leprechaun stopped the cattle stampede?

"He's done the imp pause a bull."

Lucky Clover Edition

What happened when the leprechaun fell asleep on a pile of *Green Today* magazine?

He woke up with back issues.

What were the most irrational of all the snakes St. Patrick faced?

The pi-thons.

When does the leprechaun put his car into drive?

When the light turns green, of course.

What will happen if you chop off a four-leaf clover leaf with a lawn mower?

You will likely go through a rough patch a few minutes later.

Is St. Patrick's Day fun?

It's a wonderful O'Cajun.

What happens if someone transplants your clover?

It's lawn (long) gone.

Why did the four-leaf clover cross the road?

To get to the other sod.

How can you get the wish to be immortal even though leprechauns cannot grant immortality?

Ask to be able to see the New York Yankees win a World Series.

What sign do leprechauns keep on their doormat for all to see?

"Gnome Sweet Gnome".

Lucky Clover Edition

How do clouds decorate their hair?

Rainbows.

How do you fix a broken cabbage

With a cabbage patch.

Are snakes dangerous?

Some are poisonous, but all are armless.

Riddleland

What did the gold-hungry leprechaun have for dessert?

Karrot cake.

Why do people get along so well on St. Patrick's Day?

Everyone's a green (agreeing).

When leprechaun families get together for the annual St. Patrick's celebration, what do they call it?

A wee-union.

What is the snake's favorite role model?

The librarian; she goes "Sssssssssssshhhhh" all the time.

What phrase sums up leprechauns being both practical and short?

Leprechauns are down to earth.

What do you call a mischievous sprite who pretends to have a skin disease?

A leper-con.

Lucky Clover Edition

Rather than dancing the Irish jig, what dance do pretzels prefer?

The twist.

Who recorded the history of St. Patrick driving out the snakes?

The hisssssss-torian.

What kind of gossipy book did the snake write?

A hiss-and-tell.

What do you have to decide if you come upon a four-leaf clover?

To take it or leaf it.

Why did the man with the troubled conscience decide not to take the leprechaun's gold after all?

He couldn't take gnome ore.

What color are leprechaun toilets?

They are pots of gold.

What's gold and has a head and a tail, but does not have arms, feet, or a body?

A leprechaun's gold coin.

If a leprechaun offers you three watches with the stipulation that two will bring you bad luck and one will bring you good, which watch should you take?

The third one; the third times the charm.

What do you have if you have a leprechaun that is hiding in your trailer?

A mobile gnome.

Lucky Clover Edition

What rule do leprechauns follow when crossing the street?

Only walk when the green man/green light says to walk.

Why did the leprechaun lick his fiddle?

He had good taste in music.

What kind of jokes do snakes like?

Hiss-s-s-s-s-s-s-s-sterical.

Where do most leprechauns live?

Gnome-man's Land.

What type of school did the leprechaun attend?

He was gnome-schooled.

What do you call a rainbow that is in black and white and shades of grey?

A plainbow.

What song do leprechauns sing at Christmas?

"I'll be gnome for Christmas."

What happens when a leprechaun's gold is exposed to air?

Someone tries to steal it.

Which U.S. government agency are leprechauns most likely to work in?

The Department of Gnome Land Security.

Lucky Clover Edition

Why should you NOT take a four-leaf clover for a ride in a wheelbarrow?

You should never push your luck.

What animal made a "hth hth" sound around St. Patrick?

A snake that had bit its tongue.

What kind of problem did the doctor say the leprechaun who skipped through clover had?

A gamboling problem.

Why do leprechauns argue so much with people?

They are so short they don't see eye-to-eye; in fact, they don't even see eye-to-thigh.

How do leprechaun gardeners create rich soil?

They bury their gold.

What do St. Patrick's Day and Earth Day have in common?

Everybody goes green.

Leprechauns are so small they can hide behind a mouse: what else hides behind a mouse?

Its shadow.

What were the snakes doing to cause St. Patrick to drive them out?

Putting the "hiss" in hysteria.

As they hung on the hat-rack, what did one leprechaun's hat say to his other two hats?

"I'll go on ahead; you guys keep hanging around."

Lucky Clover Edition

What did the tall four-leaf clover say to his shorter three-leafed buddies as the lawnmower approached?

I won't be long now.

Why couldn't the leprechaun cook?

His pot was full of gold.

How do leprechauns hide their gold coins?

They clover them up.

How did the barber get to the leprechaun's gold before other people?

He knew the short cuts.

How did the leprechauns greet each other on Christmas Day?

"Fairy Christmas."

What did the four-leaf clover say when weeds grew up next to it?

"Thistle be the end of me."

Where can you always find leprechauns?

In the dictionary.

Do leprechauns operate any chains of stores?

No; they only have small businesses.

What did the evil lady say when she saw the leprechaun's black cauldron at the end of the rainbow that was so similar to what the ten-year old boy said when he saw it?

The evil lady said, "I'm going to be witch" and the ten-year old boy said, "I'm going to be rich."

Lucky Clover Edition

What did the leprechaun do to win the baseball game for his team?

He hit a gnome run.

How did the leprechaun read his book?

From clover to clover.

Where is a leprechaun's favorite place to hide?

Wherever he thinks you won't find him.

What happens if you transplant a field of clover?

You may start a turf war.

Do you think green is a beautiful color?

I do; I like it as much as I like blue and yellow combined.

How do you describe a world in which everything is various shades of green?

A pigment of your imagination.

People are supposed to wear green on St. Patrick's Day; can you tell the difference between red and green?

I'm glad you can; I've noticed that many drivers at traffic lights cannot.

What happened when the four-leaf clover turned an unhealthy shade of green?

Its mom took it to the doctor.

What did the boy leprechaun say to the girl leprechaun to let her know he was fond of her?

"I am over the rainbow for you."

Lucky Clover Edition

How did the optimist leprechaun always like to end his songs?

On a high note.

What is the difference between coins and cabbages?

Coins have a head and a tail; cabbages just have a head.

How does Mother Nature package a thunderstorm?

She wraps it up with a rainbow.

How do leprechauns make a proposal?

"Wee, the people, . . . "

Why shouldn't you feel sorry for the leprechaun that tried to jump onto a passing dog but missed?

It was his own vault.

What did the leprechaun tell the children was at the end of the rainbow when he did away with a cauldron of gold and replaced it with a toilet at the end of the rainbow?

"Potty gold."

What is the leprechaun's favorite ride at the amusement park?

The fairy-go-round.

What takes place when two leprechauns meet at a cafe for coffee?

A lot of small talk.

What is it called when a leprechaun spends 24 straight hours having fun in a meadow?

A field day.

Lucky Clover Edition

What will happen if you place a four-leaf clover between the pages of a book?

You will be pressing your luck.

What is the leprechauns favorite sport?

Golf; they especially like the green.

To what did the jig-dancing foot-stomping leprechaun credit his dancing success?

His sole.

Do gardeners who grow clovers ever give up the quest to grow a four-leaf clover?

No; they just recede (reseed).

How do leprechauns spot a spy?

They let him follow them through poison ivy.

What is another name for the fake gold – fool's gold – that the leprechauns will try to sell you?

Sham rock.

Do leprechauns like to run or dance?

Dance; they would rather jig than jog.

What kind of music do leprechauns dance their jig to?

Shamrock and roll.

With all its shoes being used as good luck charms, what did the sock-footed horse feel like as he was walking around the barnyard in front of the other animals?

A foal (fool).

Lucky Clover Edition

How do you best describe a snake with no clothes?

Sssss-naked.

Why are green beverages so popular on St. Patrick's Day?

They are pitcher perfect.

What's better than finding a heads-up gold coin?

Finding two heads-up gold coins.

What adage is proven if two leprechaun cooks are seen arguing over how to make Irish stew, and the resulting product was terrible?

Two mini cooks spoil the broth.

Leprechauns are small enough to hide behind a three-leaf clover, so why do they typically hide behind four-leaf clovers?

They need all the luck they can find.

Why didn't the jealous girl get pinched on St. Patrick's Day even though she didn't wear green?

Everyone could see she was green with envy.

Why should horseshoes, rabbits' feet, and four-leaf clovers never be ironed?

You don't want to press your luck.

What kind of dog can sniff out four-leaf clovers which are about to sprout?

A budhound.

What did the snake give to his wife right before St. Patrick drove him out of Ireland?

A goodbye hiss.

Lucky Clover Edition

What do you call leprechauns who recycle?

Wee-cyclers.

How much motivation do people need to wear green on St. Patrick's Day?

Just a pinch.

Why are Irish pubs where leprechauns drink rated so poorly?

The bar is set low.

Can you count on a leprechaun to be there in tough times even if you aren't wearing green?

They'll be there in a pinch.

As you go through life, are you surprised at how little people change?

It shouldn't really be a surprise; it is the same way we do except their clothes are a whole lot tinier.

What do you call leprechaun police officers?

Under-clover cops.

What Irish dance is done in honor of tools?

The thing-a-ma-jig.

As St. Patrick led the snakes out of Ireland, what did the head snake say to the others?

"You can't venom all."

Why aren't snakes trustworthy?

They speak with a forked tongue.

Lucky Clover Edition

Are leprechauns deep thinkers?

No. The only thing on most of their minds is their hats.

Where does the zombie leprechaun keep his gold?

At the end of the brain-bowl.

Why did the police officer arrest the leprechaun?

He kept pinching.

Riddleland

Did St. Patrick think he could trust anything that a talking frog said to him?

No. He thought they put the "fib" in amphibian.

What do you call a small, cowardly piece of gold that hides at the bottom of the leprechaun's pot?

A chicken nugget.

Why do leprechauns wear green?

So they can sneak across pool tables. (Ever seen a leprechaun on a pool table? I thought not.)

What is the leprechaun's favorite part of driving on the American highway?

Going on the cloverleafs.

Which animal doesn't have rabbits' feet but is still known for its luck?

The lucky duck.

What did the shoe-making leprechaun say when he had to sneeze?

"Aaa-shoe!"

Lucky Clover Edition

What kind of fish lives in the leprechaun's pot at the end of the rainbow?

A goldfish.

Which of the shoe-making leprechauns is known for gossiping?

The one with the loose tongue.

Why did the leprechaun put his gold coins in the freezer?

He wanted cold hard cash.

What did it prove when St. Patrick's walking stick, which he always pushed into the ground when he stopped to talk, grew into an ash tree one day because he talked so long?

Even nature rooted for him.

Where do police officers put naughty rainbows?

In prism.

How did St. Patrick check to see if he was seeing an infant snake or an adult snake?

He looked for a rattle.

What did the leprechaun shoemaker who wanted to be a comedian do?

Cobbled together some jokes.

Why didn't the cook put the peach cobbler into the oven?

It's awfully hot in that oven for the leprechaun to be making shoes out of peaches.

What happens when a leprechaun goes to a job interview and mentions his height as an advantage?

He sells himself short.

Lucky Clover Edition

How do leprechauns greet each other?

"Small world, isn't it?"

What holiday do cats and dogs celebrate on March 17?

St. Pet Tricks Day.

How is the new student like a leprechaun?

Both are known for being green.

What would you call St. Patrick's walking stick if it made him rush off places?

His hurry-cane.

How did the grouchy leprechaun grant the wish?

Slowly but surly.

What do you call a chicken carrying a four-leaf clover in its beak?

The cluck of the Irish.

What do you call a mobile home - a pile of dirt on three wheels - for leprechauns?

A wheel-burrow.

How is a good joke book like a four-leaf clover?

They are hard to find and you feel lucky that you have it.

What did the leprechaun cobbler do when the man's pants covered his shoes?

Cut him some slacks.

Lucky Clover Edition

Why did the leprechaun consider trading his gold coins for Japanese currency?

He had a craving for it, a yen.

What do you call a woman who is 80% Irish?

Iris.

Why did St. Patrick keep the snakes away from caffeine?

He didn't want them to get viper active.

What's at the end of the rainbow?

It depends on which end you start - Violet is at the top end; red is on the bottom end.

FUN FACTS FOR ST PATRICK'S DAY

Where is the best place to live on St. Patrick's Day?

This depends on your point of view, but if you live in Ireland, St. Patrick's Day is a national holiday. So, people get the day off work, and children get the day off school on March 17th.

Do you know what the Irish Prime Minister gives to the US President around St. Patrick's Day?

A crystal bowl containing live shamrocks, to represent close ties between Ireland and the US.

LEAF TWO
Puns

"Don't throw away luck on little stuff.
Save it up." ~ **Tim O'Brien**

Puns are fun. They allow the speaker to express two or more meanings simultaneously. For instance, I may tell you I am feeling a little green toward St. Patrick's Day. You will likely interpret that to mean that I am going to wear the color green. You may also interpret that to mean that I am a rookie, somebody who is still learning; this meaning emerges because many fruits are green before they are ripe. If you stopped at the first meaning, you would have been right, but by going on to the second meaning you realized I was conveying a second statement as well. You could also interpret "a little green" to mean "feeling sick" or "slightly jealous."

Each of the following jokes are puns. That is, the answer has two or more ways that it can be taken. See if you can identify all the meanings. It may be funny the first time around; it may be even funnier the second time.

Lucky Clover Edition

How much does a rainbow weigh?

I'm not sure, but it is pretty light.

What happened when the leprechaun granted wishes in Spanish?

He granted uno and dos, but then he disappeared without a trace.

What happens if you find a four-leaf clover in a patch of poison ivy?

You'll have a rash of good luck.

Leprechauns will grant wishes in exchange for their freedom if captured - but the wishes do not always play out as the asker expects; is asking the leprechaun for long arms a good idea?

It has long-reaching effects.

What did the leprechaun say to the boy who wished to be a leprechaun and told the leprechaun, "I wish I were you"?

The leprechaun replied, "Change the alphabet? Very well."

Is Ireland's population growing?

Its capital is Dublin (doubling).

Leprechauns don't have to give any wishes but tend to start by offering three wishes; so why do they tend to bargain beginning with three wishes?

I guess they are willing to try (tri).

What did St. Patrick conclude once the snakes presented their case to stay in Ireland?

He determined they didn't have a leg to stand on.

Lucky Clover Edition

Where is the angriest place on earth?

Ire Land.

How did the cobbler make money from shoes other people considered to be trash?

He resoled them.

What do you call a leprechaun that runs around naked in public?

A lucky streaker.

Why did the boy think St. Patrick had a car?

He heard St. Patrick drove the snakes out of Ireland.

Why are leprechauns regarded as environmentalists?

They like being green.

What do dwarves, elves, gnomes, leprechauns, and imps all have in common?

When you get right down to it, they have very little.

What is a leprechaun's favorite soft drink?

Sprite.

How is a shoe-making leprechaun like a pie?

They are both cobblers.

What do you call the leprechaun who was in a hurry to see a doctor, and rushed into the doctor's office, demanding to see the doctor immediately?

He was a little imp-patient.

Lucky Clover Edition

Why did the mischievous leprechaun turn the bodybuilder into a rowboat?

The body builder had wished to be in ship shape.

Why did the leprechaun play his fiddle inside the refrigerator?

He wanted to play cool tunes.

How much of the leprechaun's money does the skunk want?

One scent.

Riddleland

Why do leprechauns cheer for rookies?

Rookies are known to be green.

Why was the Irish boy carrying the pointed cyclical toy down to breakfast?

Because it was the top of the morning.

What condition are the coins in the leprechaun's pot of gold?

Mint.

Who invented the Irish jig dance?

Someone waiting for a turn in the restroom.

How do you best describe the funk of a leprechaun who broods, complains, and worries?

Irish stew.

What happened after the golfer's ball landed in a patch of four-leaf clovers?

The golfer had a stroke of good luck.

Lucky Clover Edition

Why did the leprechaun fall into the well?

He couldn't see that well.

How did the leprechaun feel watching his shoes get smashed by the trash compactor?

It was sole-crushing.

Do violin-playing leprechauns do a lot of hard work?

No, they fiddle around a lot.

Why didn't St. Patrick trust the large worm-like creatures that were around him?

He thought they were snakes in the grass.

What's the difference between doing a jig and tap dancing?

You don't risk falling into the sink when you dance a jig.

If you catch a leprechaun, he will propose giving you three wishes in exchange for his freedom. What do you think of that number?

It sounds odd to me.

What did people worry would happen when the boy spoke and brought his rabbit-good-luck charm up to his lips?

They worried he would put his foot in his mouth.

Why do soldiers really enjoy St. Patrick's Day?

Because it's in the middle of a long March.

How did people know the horse was sad when the farmer took one of its shoes for good luck?

It had a long face.

Lucky Clover Edition

What did the leprechaun say after he was pickpocketed?

"How could anyone stoop so low?"

Why did the leprechaun keep a rowboat?

He knew gold was found in oars.

What shade of green are the leprechauns' submarines?

Sublime.

What bank can you go to, possibly find gold, take the gold, and not get arrested?

A riverbank.

How did the girl know a leprechaun was hiding somewhere in the shopping center?

She saw the mall larky.

Why should you never marry a leprechaun?

Most of them are gold diggers.

Did St. Patrick resort to trickery to get the snakes to leave Ireland?

No; the snakes didn't have a leg to pull.

What is the name of that huge black pot containing the leprechaun's gold at the end of the rainbow?

It's called Ron (cauldron).

How did it go when the leprechaun searched for gold at the riverbank?

It didn't pan out.

Lucky Clover Edition

What happened when the two leprechauns got thirsty overnight?

They had to make dew.

What do you call the books St. Patrick read for his personal spiritual growth?

Cross reference.

Why was the baker searching for the leprechaun's gold?

He needed some extra dough.

Why did the football coach go looking for the leprechaun's money?

He was hoping to find at least a quarterback.

Did you realize a leprechaun's mine can have only gold or silver but not both?

It's either ore.

Who does a leprechaun take his bowler hat off to?

The barber.

What is the fear of getting pinched on St. Patrick's Day for not wearing green?

Claws-trophobia.

Why did the crab want to get all the leprechaun's gold and keep it for himself?

He was shellfish.

Is it reasonable for a leprechaun to keep a machine that turns his gold into coins?

It makes cents.

Lucky Clover Edition

What did the shoe-making leprechaun say to the fly?

"Shoo."

Why did the leprechaun wipe off the coil?

He was doing his spring cleaning.

What beverage does a leprechaun like to order at a Chinese restaurant?

Green tea.

What did the goo-goo eyed boy tell the girl in addition to the fact that the horseshoe was his favorite charm?

"I'm in love with the shape of U."

What fast food beverage sounds like an Irish Dance?

The Shamrock Shake.

How did the snakes react to being booted out of Ireland?

They had a hissy fit.

How are some jokes like the leprechaun's bowler hat?

They go over your head.

What did the gold hunter say when asked how he was feeling?

"I'm not feeling two grand yet."

Is it okay to be prejudiced against leprechauns?

Leprechauns may be short, but that's no reason to look down on them.

Lucky Clover Edition

How is a gardener and a leprechaun alike?

Both have green thumbs.

What did the leprechaun call the music playing from the device inside his pillowcase?

Sham rock.

What did the shoe-making leprechaun say to the other when he got mad?

"Hey; keep hold of your tongue."

Why aren't there any videos of leprechauns playing their fiddle?

Leprechauns don't like fiddling with a camera.

Why do certain leprechauns know where the four-leaf clovers are and others don't?

It's on a need to mow basis.

What did the leprechaun do when he was sawing down a four-leaf clover and a human started to walk toward him?

He had to cut it short.

What do you call clovers that are older than you are?

Pasturage.

Do leprechauns make fascinating shoes?

Try a pair; you'll be tripping.

What do you say to an impatient person as you try to remove a shoe from his horses for good luck?

"Hold your horses."

Lucky Clover Edition

Why did the Irish boy think his Irish potato had been imported?

His mom said it had been cooked in Greece.

Why did the leprechaun wear a bowler hat day after day instead of changing to a ballcap?

His caps lock was on.

Why can you never borrow gold or money from a leprechaun?

Leprechauns always claim they are a little short.

Riddleland

Did you hear about the man who wished to a leprechaun for a job where he could be seen with pride?

The leprechaun made him a lion tamer.

Why did the restaurant which featured leprechauns as waiters have such poor service?

They were short staffed.

How do female leprechauns (some people say these are actually "sprites" and there is no such thing as a female leprechaun; there are only male leprechauns) - wear their hair?

In pixie cuts.

Do you believe that if you kiss the Blarney stone you will have good luck?

I think it's a rocky investment.

What is it called when leprechauns have a party?

A little get together.

Lucky Clover Edition

What's green and not heavy?

Light green.

How are people who watch for people dressed in green like an Irish potato?

Both keep their eyes peeled.

How do we know leprechauns are bright people?

There are lots of them that are out standing in their field.

What happened when St. Patrick could not lead worship because of the snakes crawling around?

It was mass hiss-teria.

What do all stories about rainbows have?

An arc.

Which baseball league do leprechauns play in?

Little League.

Lucky Clover Edition

Why don't witches wear round hats like leprechauns?

They see no point to them.

What is the leprechaun's butt called?

A fairy tail.

How are whiney violins and hot-tempered leprechauns alike?

Both are high strung.

Does wearing a bowler hat and a suit help keep leprechauns alive?

It minimizes casual tees.

What do you call a little Irish potato?

A small fry.

Do four-leaf clovers feel pain if plucked?

They mown (moan).

Lucky Clover Edition

What kind of literature do leprechauns like to read?

Short stories.

How is the leprechaun's fiddle like a disgusting motel?

Both are vile inns.

What kind of jokes do snakes like best?

S-s-s-s-s-s-s-s-s-s-s-silly S-s-s-s-s-s-s-s-s-s-scenarios.

Ireland is known for its potatoes, but the first potato may not have been cooked in Ireland. Where were they likely cooked?

In Greece.

Some leprechauns are mean and like to insult people, while others are very, very happy; how can you describe both groups at the same time?

They like to be little people.

What kind of Irish potato lays around on the sofa all day?

The couch potato.

How did the leprechaun make gold soup?
He put in 24 carrots.

FUN FACTS FOR ST PATRICK'S DAY

How many people do you think have Irish roots in America?

34.8 million. That is more than 7 times the population of Ireland.

Do you think St. Patrick's Day is celebrated around the world?

It most definitely is. In 2019, over 300 different stadiums, statues, towers, and well-known tourist sites such as the Sydney Opera House in Australia, The Burj Al Arab in United Arab Emirates, the Leaning Tower of Pisa in Italy, the Statue of Christ the Redeemer in Rio de Janeiro, all went green for St. Patrick's Day.

LEAF THREE
Silly Scenarios and Words of Wisdom

"For the whole world is Irish on the seventeenth o' March!" ~ **Thomas Augustine Daly**

Legends about St. Patrick abound; people loved to tell stories back in the Middle Ages. In fact, in the days before the printing press, printed documents were scarce, and therefore the only way to pass around material among one's friends or to pass it down to one's children was to tell it. Stories were a lot of fun to tell and to hear - and they were very memorable.

I'm sure you probably like to tell stories too; I know I do. Here are several humorous stories and words of wisdom focused on St. Patrick's Day:

I've heard the saying "You can't judge a book by its cover" many times, but when looking for the perfect spot to fish, I just learned **"You can't judge a brook by its clover"** too.

A leprechaun approached a cobbler who was working on a pair of boots. "What are you making?" the leprechaun called, unable to see the boots. The cobbler replied, "A shoe."
Still struggling to see what the cobbler was making, the leprechaun said, "Bless you; that was a horrible sneeze. Now, please tell me what you are making?"

Some St. Patrick's Day trivia: Just because a frog is green does not mean that it is Irish.
In fact, as babies, most frogs look a tad Polish.

"Help! Help! A deadly snake is after me," a camper called as he tried to stay ahead of a six-foot black snake that was slithering quickly behind him. A counselor looked up from where he sat in a folding chair reading and said calmly, "Black snakes aren't poisonous. The only poisonous snakes around here are cottonmouths and copperheads. Black snakes aren't deadly."
"What do you mean this snake is not deadly? He's going to chase me off a cliff."

Lucky Clover Edition

Walking through the meadow one day, I saw the scroungiest leprechaun I have ever seen in my life. He was mud covered; his once-impressive clothes were torn. Curious, I decided to strike a conservation. "If you don't mind my asking, what happened to you? I thought leprechauns had neatly pressed green suits and green bowlers; that you carried instruments like fiddles wherever you went; that you had pots of gold that you guarded; and that you could do magic."

The leprechaun brushed himself off and said, "I was the typical leprechaun until about fifteen minutes ago. I was in the meadow playing my fiddle while guarding my gold when a big dog snuck upon me. I dropped my instrument in fear and ran; the dog chased me, and I fell into the mud. I was so nervous that I didn't use my magic. The dog grabbed me, tossed me around, and dropped me into the river. I floated downstream, snagging my clothes. Now here I am, with ruined clothes, no magic, no gold, and no musical instrument."

"What's your name?"

"Lucky."

One day a leprechaun got lost and wandered into an office. A man looked up from his desk, saw the leprechaun, and snatched him. The leprechaun introduced himself and offered the man three wishes in exchange for his freedom. The man loosened his grip and agreed to the deal.

"What's your first wish?" the leprechaun asked, anxious to get the deal done. "I want a world without lawyers," the man said, thinking of all the legal issues he had.

Poof! All the lawyers were removed from the world, including those down the hall in the legal office. As the man looked at the empty legal office, the leprechaun squirmed, got out of the man's grasp, and started to walk away.

"What about my other two wishes?" the man demanded, reaching but failing to grasp the leprechaun.

"Sue me," teased the leprechaun as he scampered to safety.

Lucky Clover Edition

Leprechauns will grant wishes in exchange for their freedom to anyone who captures them - but leprechauns are tricksters who fulfill the wish but not in the way the recipient intended. For instance, Joe and Paul were two college professors at a small university. One day they saw a leprechaun as they walked across campus, and a wild chase ensued. Eventually, they trapped the leprechaun in a corner of a classroom. Fearing for his life, the leprechaun offered them each one wish in exchange for his freedom. Both Joe and Paul were young professors, and so Joe said, "I want to be Chair of the English Department" and Paul followed suit, saying, "I want to be made Chair of the Math Department."

Poof! Their wish was granted - but not the way they had intended. Joe found himself as a plush chair in the English department's conference room and Paul found himself as a folding chair in the Math department's faculty lounge.

Their wives eventually realized what had happened and took the two chairs to the doctor's office to see what could be done. The doctor asked for a few minutes to be alone with the chairs. Upon returning from his examination, the doctor was asked by the wives, "How are our husbands? Are they in pain?"

The doctor paused and thoughtfully said, "They're both quite comfortable."

Lucky Clover Edition

Three friends, Tom, Dick, and Harry, are walking through a green meadow returning from a fishing trip empty-handed when suddenly they come upon a leprechaun. Thinking quickly, Tom tosses the fishing net over the leprechaun and says, "I bet he can grant wishes."

"No way," the others say in unison.

"Five dollars says he can!" Tom stated boldly and shook hands with the other two boys.

"I can do wishes," the leprechaun stated confidently. "I normally grant three wishes to anyone that catches me, but, since there are three of you, I will make you a deal – in exchange for my freedom, I will grant you each a wish.

"This is bogus," Harry exclaimed. "It's a trick to make us let him out of the net." The leprechaun remained calm and asked, "What's your wish, big mouth?"

"Okay, I'll play your silly game. I want to go to my grandma's house in Ireland," he said, and, as soon as he said it, he was gone. Amazed, Dick said, "I want to be on a tropical island with a pot of gold."

No sooner had he said it, he was gone.

"And for you?" the leprechaun asked as Tom released him from the net. "I wish those two cheapskates were back here; they owe me five dollars!"

(Do this one with a friend; you read the dark part and they will automatically say the light part.)

Are you a potato? Let's find out!

Okay.

Can we agree that potatoes have skin?

Yes.

Can we agree that potatoes have eyes?

Yes.

Do you have skin?

Yes.

Do you have eyes?

Yes.

Then you must be a potato. And you know what?

What?

I'm glad that we're best spuds!

FUN FACTS FOR ST PATRICK'S DAY

Do you know who connected to St. Patrick's Day, was kidnapped aged 16 years old, and also worked as shepherd for six years?

This was St. Patrick himself.

Do you know why we celebrate St. Patrick's Day on the 17th of March?

This was said to be the day that he died, most likely in 461.

LEAF FOUR
Knock-Knock Jokes

"May your troubles be less. And your blessings be more. And nothing but happiness come through your door." ~ **Irish blessing**

If you are in the meadow catching bugs and you accidently capture a leprechaun, the leprechaun is going to knock-knock on your container to get your attention so that you will let him out. In the spirit of that knocking, here are 25 knock knock jokes centered around St. Patrick's Day.

KNOCK, KNOCK.
Who's there?
Ireland.
Ireland who?
Ireland a few pinches - I promise it won't hurt - on your arm if you don't wear green.

Lucky Clover Edition

KNOCK, KNOCK.
Who's there?
Saint.
Saint who?
Saint it wonderful to be telling knock-knock jokes again.

KNOCK, KNOCK.
Who's there?
Irish.
Irish who?
Irish you a Happy St. Patrick's Day.

KNOCK, KNOCK.
Who's there?
Miss Chief.
Miss Chief who?
Miss Chief is something leprechauns like to do, and it gets them in trouble.

KNOCK, KNOCK.
Who's there?
A Green.
A Green who?
A Green (agreeing) that St. Patrick's Day is a fun day to celebrate.

KNOCK, KNOCK.
Who's there?
Otis.
Otis who?
Otis is a bunch of fun.

KNOCK, KNOCK.
Who's there?
Gnome Adder.
Gnome Adder who?
Gnome Adder how many knock-knock jokes I hear, I always want to hear one more.

Lucky Clover Edition

KNOCK, KNOCK.
Who's there?
Ireland.
Ireland who?
Ireland you my pencil if you promise to give it back.

KNOCK, KNOCK.
Who's there?
Sir Pence.
Sir Pence who?
Sir Pence (serpents) were driven out of Ireland by St. Patrick.

KNOCK, KNOCK.
Who's there?
Fairy.
Fairy who?
Fairy pleased with these knock-knock jokes so far.

KNOCK, KNOCK.
Who's there?
Fairy Tail.
Fairy Tail who?
Fairy Tails usually begin, "Once upon a time."

Lucky Clover Edition

KNOCK, KNOCK.
Who's there?
Art O' Ficial.
Art O' Ficial who?
Art O' Ficial (artificial) shamrocks are okay, but I prefer real ones.

KNOCK, KNOCK.
Who's there?
Jack.
Jack who?
Jackpot is waiting under the rainbow.

KNOCK, KNOCK.
Who's there?
M.T.
M.T. who?
M.T. wallets are no fun; let's go find some leprechaun gold.

KNOCK, KNOCK.
Who's there?
Gnome Eye.
Gnome Eye who?
Gnome Eye leprechaun facts and knock-knock jokes; do you know yours?

Lucky Clover Edition

KNOCK, KNOCK.

Who's there?

Patrick.

Patrick who?

Patrick me; did Pat trick you too?

KNOCK, KNOCK.
Who's there?
Accordion.
Accordion who?
Accordion legend, leprechauns have a pot of gold at the end of the rainbow.

KNOCK, KNOCK.
Who's there?
Clara Nett.
Clara Nett who?
Clara Nett (clarinet) is an instrument some leprechauns play, but most prefer the fiddle.

KNOCK, KNOCK.
Who's there?
Wooden Shoe.
Wooden Shoe who?
Wooden Shoe like to see a leprechaun and hear more knock-knock jokes?

Lucky Clover Edition

KNOCK, KNOCK.
Who's there?
Mickey.
Mickey who?
Mickey doesn't fit your door.

KNOCK, KNOCK.
Who's there?
Clover.
Clover who?
Clover knock-knock jokes take wit to enjoy.

KNOCK, KNOCK.
Who's there?
Irish Stew.
Irish Stew who?
Irish Stew (I arrest you) in the name of the law.

KNOCK, KNOCK.
Who's there?
Fiddle.
Fiddle who?
Fiddle (if it will) be, it will be.

Lucky Clover Edition

KNOCK, KNOCK.
Who's there?
Midas.
Midas who?
Midas well tell some more knock-knock jokes; this is fun.

KNOCK, KNOCK.
Who's there?
Soup Herb.
Soup Herb who?
Soup Herb (superb) job of doing the knock-knock jokes; keep up the good work.

KNOCK, KNOCK.
Who's there?
Snakeskin.
Snakeskin who?
Snakeskin be poisonous, so be careful around them.

KNOCK, KNOCK.

Who's there?

Sir Plus.

Sir Plus who?

Sir Plus gold is available at the end of the rainbow if you get there before anyone – or anything - else.

FUN FACTS FOR ST PATRICK'S DAY

Do you know what the official symbol of Ireland is?

You would be wrong if you thought it was a shamrock. But, you'd be correct, if you said harp. It has been a key symbol of Ireland since Medieval times.

Do you know what two foods are bought in preparation for St. Patrick's Day?

Cabbages and corned beef. 26 billion pounds of beef, and 2 billion pounds of cabbage are produced during St. Patrick's Day.

Did you enjoy the book?

If you did, we are ecstatic. If not, please write your complaint to us and we will ensure we fix it.

If you're feeling generous, there is something important that you can help me with – tell other people that you enjoyed the book.

Ask a grown-up to write about it on Amazon. When they do, more people will find out about the book. It also lets Amazon know that we are making kids around the world laugh. Even a few words and ratings would go a long way.

If you have any ideas or jokes that you think are super funny, please let us know. We would love to hear from you. Our email address is - **riddleland@riddlelandforkids.com**

Riddleland

Riddleland Bonus Book

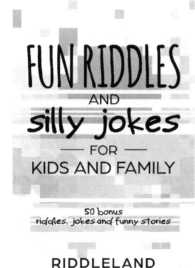

http://pixelfy.me/riddlelandbonus

Thank you for buying this book. We would like to share a special bonus as a token of appreciation. It is a collection of 50 original jokes, riddles, and two super funny stories!

Join our **Facebook Group** at **Riddleland for Kids** to get daily jokes and riddles.

Lucky Clover Edition

Would you like your jokes and riddles to be featured in our next book?

We are having a contest to see who are the smartest or funniest boys and girls in the world! :
1) **Creative and Challenging Riddles**
2) **Tickle Your Funny Bone Contest**

Parents, please email us your child's "Original" Riddle or Joke and **he or she could win a Riddleland book and be featured in our next book.**

Here are the rules:
1) It must be challenging for the riddles and funny for the jokes!
2) It must be 100% original and not something from the Internet! It is easy to find out!
3) You can submit both jokes and riddles as they are 2 separate contests.
4) No help from the parents unless they are as funny as you.
5) Winners will be announced via email or our Facebook group – Riddleland for kids
6) Please also mention what book you purchased.
7) Email us at Riddleland@riddlelandforkids.com

Other Fun Books for Kids!

Riddles Series

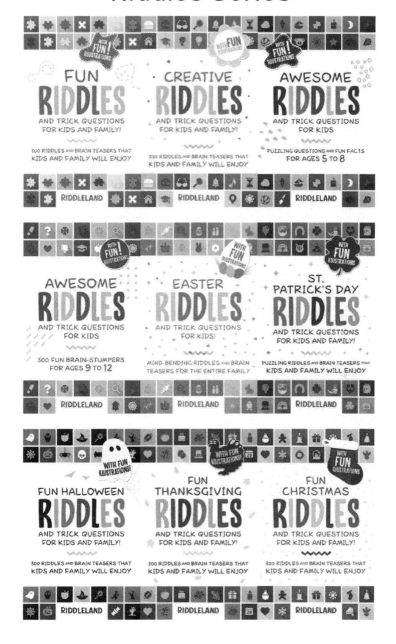

Riddleland

It's Laugh O'Clock Series

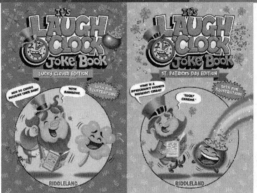

Lucky Clover Edition

It's Laugh O'Clock
Would You Rather Series

Would You Rather Series

Get them on Amazon
or our website at www.riddlelandforkids.com

About Riddleland

Riddleland is a mom + dad run publishing company. We are passionate about creating fun and innovative books to help children develop their reading skills and fall in love with reading. If you have suggestions for us or want to work with us, shoot us an email at riddleland@riddlelandforkids.com

Our family's favorite quote:

"Creativity is an area in which younger people have a tremendous advantage since they have an endearing habit of always questioning past wisdom and authority."
~ Bill Hewlett

Made in the USA
Monee, IL
09 March 2023

29482278R00059